Lessons in Poetry

Kaashvi Kumar

BookLeaf Publishing

India | USA | UK

Presentation by *BookLeaf Publishing*

Web: www.bookleafpub.com

E-mail: info@bookleafpub.com

ISBN: 9789360944971

First edition 2024

To my sister Kyra, whom I love so very much. You are the light to my darkness and the best thing that's ever happened to me.

ACKNOWLEDGEMENT

I would first like to thank my mother. She is the reason I started writing and is the reason I kept on going. Without her, none of this would have been possible. I would have never imagined writing a poetry book, but here I am. There is probably nothing in this world I could do to express my gratitude to you mumma. She was the first person to read most of my poems and has never failed to keep encouraging me to do more. For this, I thank her.

I would also like to give my thanks to my two best friends. I would first like to say thanks to a friend who kept on encouraging me to continue. She always said she was proud of me and she was always saying stuff like. 'Wow, keep it going!' or 'This is amazing.' She kept me going even when I felt like I wasn't writing well. Mihika, you are a star. I love you so much and I owe you so much! You have no idea how much those little sentences and expressions made me feel. You made me feel so happy with myself and proud of myself.

Lastly, I give my utmost thanks and gratitude to my best friend who helped me so much with what to write. Awawa, as I like to call her, was there with me for almost every step of my journey to this book. She played a huge role in the ideas part of the poems. I was stuck. I couldn't think of what to write about, but just one quick phone call to her and I already had hundreds of ideas. Well, maybe not hundreds, but enough to keep me busy for weeks. I thank you Awawa, so much!

One last person I would like to acknowledge is one of my cousins. When I first started, not many people would read my poems, but he read every single one of them and encouraged me do keep going. He would say things like 'Exquisite writing!' Or 'Keep them rolling'. These short sentences did a lot to boost my motivation and I thank him for that.

PREFACE

These poems reflect on the experiences in my life and how life can sometimes be complicated. They tell us that our darkest moments are parts of what makes us who we are. They may play a large role in who we are or a small role, but regardless, each moment shapes us. These poems are not only about life or love, but they also have meaning. Each verse, each stanza, means something much deeper. Poems are not just descriptions wrapped around with pretty words, but riddles that mean so much more.

As Dawn Emerges...

In the canvas of dawn, a spectacle spun,

A masterpiece painted by the rising sun.

Horizon ablaze in hues of gold,

A tale of warmth and promises told.

The night surrenders, stars take flight,

As the sun ascends with radiant might.

A symphony of colors, a celestial hymn,

A herald of hope as the day begins.

On the edge of darkness, a golden kiss,

Illuminating landscapes with gentle bliss.

Mountains and valleys bathed in light,

A resurrection from the tranquil night.

The world awakens, a sleepy yawn,

As the sun unveils the secrets drawn.

Casting shadows that dance and play,

In the soft glow of the morning's ray.

A celestial journey, day after day,

The sun rises in its grand display.

A beacon of life, a symbol of mirth,

A testament to the vastness of the Earth.

So, let the sun ascend, let it rise,

Chasing away the night's disguise.

A promise etched in the morning sky,

A new beginning as the sun draws night.

Love's celestial ballet

Under the silver canopy of the night,

Stars ignite the sky with a gentle light,

A tale is created, woven soft and tight,

Of love's embrace, a celestial rite.

In whispers shared beneath the crescent moon,

Two hearts converge, an eternal tune,

A serenade of love, a sweet monsoon,

Where passion flows, a tranquil dune.

Through valleys low and mountains high,

Journeys unfold, painting the sky,

A palette of emotions, where spirits fly,

In the language of love, we amplify.

A tender touch, a language so pure,

A gentle caress, emotions assure.

In the Gallery of hearts, love's art matures,

A masterpiece invented, forever secure.

Like petals unfurling in the morning light,

Love blossoms, a flower so pure and bright.

Through twilight shadows and morning's flight.

A feeling remains an everlasting sight.

Through the tapestry of joy and tears,

Love perseveres, conquering fears,

In the echo of laughter, where happiness steers,

Love whispers promises in the attentive ears.

So let love be the compass, our guiding star

Through galaxies of joy, and valleys far.

In the dance of love, wherever we are.

For in the universe's grand ballet,

Love remains constant, come what may,

A sonnet of the heart, a serenade to convey,

For in the arms of love, we eternally stay.

The dance of cricket

In green meadows, where shadows play,

A game unfurls, where willows sway,

In a yellow-tinted field, a wicket stands,

Cricket's dance, in distant lands.

Beneath the azure masterpiece, skies so high,

A gentle breeze, a heartfelt sigh,

Stalwart players on rough ground,

The traditional song, a sweet sound

The bat ascends, a gracefully powerful stroke,

A rhythmic and swift dance, like smoke,

The ball, a swift ballet,

In tandem with the sun's display

Stumps in line, a castle fair,

Defenders strive, the bails in the air,

The bowler's art, a craft refined,

A silent battle waged in the air and mind

Ode to boundaries, a four's embrace,

A six that soars, invoking a thrilling chase.

In cricket's realm, the scorecard's tale,

A saga spun, a riveting trail.

Amidst the cheers and fervent cries,

Legends rise beneath their watchful eyes,

A test of patience, timeless grace,

One Day's Dash, a sprinting race

On verdant fields, a sport so grand,

Where nations meet, and brotherhood stand,

In cricket's heart, a unity,

A global tapestry, diverse and free

So let the Willow sing its tune,

Beneath the radiant, watching moon,

In cricket's spirit, hearts align,

A timeless game, forever divine.

Our Friendship

Beneath the Willow's weeping boughs,

Where whispers dance, soft promises avow,

A legend unfolds, sparked in the hush of the glade,

Where shadows linger and secrets fade.

Where moonlight carves pathways and stars align,

In a celestial ballet, an intricate design,

Footprints etched on sands of time,

Each mark, a gentle chime.

A language unspoken, yet deeply known,

In the heart's sanctuary, seeds are sown,

In the realm of happiness, a tale unfolds,

Two souls interconnected, their story unfolds.

In twilight's embrace, shadows meld,

Kindred spirits, an unspoken trend,

Palettes of emotions, splashed in the night,

In the quiet canvas, an unbreakable bond takes flight.

On the river's edge, reflections gleam,

A shared journey, a silent dream.

The ripples tell of mystic stories untold,

In the silent echoes, friendship unfolds.

In the melody of rustling leaves,

A covenant made, the heart believes,

Through the echoes of laughter, so clear,

Whispers of promises made only for friends to hear.

Let the tapestry of silence weave,

In the sacred stillness, our bonds achieve,

For in the mute spaces, the truth resides,

And in the unspoken, friendship shall abide.

Nature's Gift

Beneath God's watchful gaze and the vast sky,

Where Cerulean meets an ocean's sigh,

A world of mystery and wonder lies below,

In depths, where mystic currents flow

The ocean's dance, a symphonic tide,

A timeless waltz, far and wide,

Every wave, a whisper of tales,

Of ancient ships and seafarer's trail

Sunset splashes across the sea,

Unknown strokes of paint,

Reflections dance on liquid glass,

As daylight melts, the shadows pass

The world under, secrets keep

A realm where creatures peacefully sleep,

From vibrant reefs to hidden coves,

A melody of life unfolds.

Majestic whales, their voices low,

Echo through the waters,

Their voices far far below,

Dolphins dance in joyful delight,

Underneath the pale moonlight.

Seagulls soar on salty breeze,

Guided discreetly by distant seas,

A rounded shape, left behind on sandy shores,

Witness to the ever-changing mores.

Storms rage with furious might,

Yet, the tranquil moments trail the night,

Moonlight's kiss on midnight waves,

A gentle lullaby the ocean craves.

Beneath constellations of stars, a silver sheen,

A cosmic dance, a celestial dream,

Our ocean's heartbeat, a constant drum,

Connecting me and you, they to them,

Stand upon the shore and see,

The never-ending horizon, wild and free,

For in the ocean's ebb and flow,

A timeless beauty starts to grow.

Life's defiance

In the grand theatre, we call our life, a script unfolds,
A detailed dance of fables, hidden and untold,
Yet fairness, a phantom, elusive and sly,
Leaves some in darkness, we question why.

Underneath the moon's soft silvery glow,
Where some hearts rejoice, others sorrow
A celestial ballet with steps uneven,
This unfurls Life's unfair choreography, a tale of reason

He toils with dreams so vast,
Yet barriers rise, and obstacles cast,
Pulling him down,
Down, into the depths where shadows frown.

In the market square, where prized fortunes sway,
Some find abundance, while others find dismay,
Weaving destiny's tapestry, threads so very thin,
Unfair hands dealt, a game we are in.

Yet, within the shadows, a group of resilience thrives,

A silent, yet dangerous protest, as hope survives,
For when in your heart's chamber, a flame
lights,
Defying unfairness, as compassion ignites

Through our valleys of despair and peaks so
very high,
In unity, we find out strength to defy,
When injustice may linger, a constant dare,
Together we rise, a collective prayer

Tales of the Unfavoured

In a house, where shadows dance

A perfect family takes its chance

Of favouritism, subtle but bold

A story of love begins to unfold

In the corner, a family frame

A child basks in love's sweet flame

Her laughter, now echoing through the hall

Is soon replaced, her happiness now small

She, who was once bathed in attention, now a silent muse

Now in shadows, cast by life's relentless cruise

A tale of neglect whispered from within the
night

Her heartache, hidden from plain sight

parent's eyes fixed on the small

The youngest one, a favoured thrall

Attention flows like a gentle stream

While she becomes one of distant dreams

Oh the burden of love, so unfairly unequal

A weight upon her heart, so feeble

The favoured, a cherished gem

Leaving her in the shadows, condemned

Yet, within the tapestry of uneven grace,

Lies a lesson for the human race,

To see the worth in every soul,

No matter the age or the tale they unroll

For love should bloom in equal measure,

In the heart of every family's treasure,

Let her find solace's wing,

And let her joy and worth both sing

In the end, let compassion reign,

And ment the bonds that bear her strain,

For when together, families thrive in love's light,

It illuminates the child, both day and night

The waves of freedom

On the shore, where majestic waves kiss the
land,
I gently plant my feet, enjoying the cool sand,
I feel the sun beating down my back, warming
my skin,
I taste a salty breeze, that whispers secrets
within.

I hear the seagulls squawk overhead, their cries
claiming the sky,
I see the waves roll in, saying 'hi' and 'bye',
No formalities are found just nature's show,
Where the tides come and the tides go.

I see footprints in the sand, my tiny trail,
It's like a story written, but one without fail,
I see the sun, its colours bursting out and
painting the water in an orange shade,
I see the birds as they finally start to fade.

I hear kids squealing, building castles with glee,
I see them collect shells, those tiny treasures of
the sea,
I see the beachcombers, their spirits at play,

I see them play, underneath the sun's relentless
display.

I see the driftwood, standing like ancient
sentinels,
Their curved branches imitate large tentacles,

A Sky of wonder

Beneath the inky black cosmic sheet,
Where stars and stories come to meet,
Constellations, like graffiti in the night,
Swirled around across the universe, a piece of
pure delight.

Leo roars, a majestic feline king,
In the midnight darkness, his praises sing,
Mane made of starlight, a regal sight,
He rules the celestial jungle with his might.

The pegasus soars, a winged horse on high,
Cantering through the astral canvas,
With constellations as his mane,
He gallops through the cosmos, free from rein.

Sagittarius, with his bow, aims with glee,
An archer, wild and free,
Arrows of stardust, flies with precision,
In the vastness of space, a glorious expedition,

The Pleiades, an interstellar sisterhood,
Seven diamonds in the cosmic woods.
Twinkling and dancing, a heavenly spree,

A sisterly bond, one for all to see

As I lay beneath the night's dark shroud,
I gaze up at the constellations, standing bold and
proud,
In the vast expanse of this infinite sea,
Let their informal tales set our spirits free

The Ebony Elegance

In the corner, a masterpiece takes its stand,
A companion with keys, weathered and grand,
Taking my seat, fingers itching to play,
A casual chat, in a musical way.

Ivory, like old buddies, conducts tales of the
past,
White keys create a base and black keys add
spice, a contrast so vast,
Copper vibrates against the bridge, each hit a
soft tune,
A rhythm unfolds, the notes floating underneath
the dim moon.

Fingers tap and notes response,
In this casual jam, a bond is spawned,
This silent room slowly fills with memories,
happy and blue,
A musical conversation, between me and you.

No fancy symphony needed, just a soft melody,
The piano and I, living harmoniously,
In this musical banter, we find our groove,
In a laid-back duet, the instrument and I move.

From jazz to pop, it's a passionate ride,
The piano and I, together, side by side,
The chords ascend and descend, resonating a
musical rollercoaster,
Fire ignites around and I realize the end has
never been closer.

A fantasy World

In a corner, a cup in hand,
I dive into a world of books, like walking on
sand,
Coffee stains the creme pages,
In a world of stories, time engages.

Paperback covers, creased and worn,
Each tale is like a journey, a new dawn,
Where lights flicker in a cozy nook,
Every plot twist is like a sly hook.

Characters speak, an language unknown,
In this literary chaos, I know I'm not alone,
Surrounded by dusty shelves and comfy chairs,
I'm lost in a fantasy world, blissfully unaware

The joy of christmas

'Twas the night before Christmas, through the place,
With excitement growing, and a grin on each face,
Stockings were hung by the fireplace with flair,
In hopes that ol' Santa Claus would be there.

When out on the lawn, there arose much clatter,
Springing from the couch, I dash to see the matter,
Away from the window, I dance like a flash,
Tore the blinds into two, threw up the sash,

The moon on the snow gave a bluish sheen,
Gave the lustre of midday to objects unseen,
When, what to my wondering eyes should appear,
But a miniature sleigh, and 8 tiny reindeer.

With a little old driver, so lively and quick,
I knew in a moment, it could only be Saint Nick!
Faster than rapid eagles, his coursers they came,
And he whistled and shouted, calling their name.

'Now Dasher, now Dancer, now Prancer and
Vixen!'
'And Comet, and Cupid, and Donner and
Blitzen.'
'To the top, the top of the porch, to the top of the
wall,'
'Now dash away, dash away, dash away all.'

The glory of Swimming

Beneath the sunlit sky, in a place where water
gleams,
I dive into the pool, chasing liquid dreams,
With every stroke, I abandon the world behind,
In the cool embrace of the water, solace I find.

In the water's symphony, with a splash and a
sigh,
It reflects the rhythm of my spirit's reply.
In the soft current, my worries dissolve.
As I swim through echoes, problems evolve.

The water touch on my skin, a soothing caress,
Washing away my life's tangled mess,
A liquid sanctuary, where I'm free,
At that moment, It's just the water and me

The bitter taste of chlorine, a poolside breeze,
A melody of laughter, my soul appease
With each lap, I'm a mermaid in flight,
Chasing joy in the gleaming light.

Here I am, swimming through time,
A liquid journey, both simple and sublime,
In the pool's hold, where I feel alive,
I swim through my feelings, in this aquatic dive

Musical Fantasy

In the world of melodies, where beats take flight,
Songs are magic, soft tunes tuning the night,
Guitars strum lazily, like a backyard chill,
Lyrics spill stories, giving me a thrill.

Piano keys tinkle, a playful tease,
Harmonies hugging, putting me at ease,
Hitting the play button, I let the music flow,
In the land of music, let your spirit glow.

Sing it out loud, hum it low,
In the world of tunes, let your feelings grow,
From sunrise hums to midnight tunes,
To me, every beat's a treasure, something
irreplaceable under the moon.

So let the lyrics guide you, through highs and
lows,
For songs are the medicine for life's throes,
For music is a place where everyone belongs,
Nothing could go wrong.

First Day Back

Sunrise whispers, a 'brand new day,'
First steps back into high school, no time to
delay,
With my backpack loaded, my heart flutters,
A journey ahead, like melted butter.

Hallways are like mazes, with twists and turns,
Lost in the labyrinth, my stomach churns,
Seniors strutting, like they own the place,
I'm just someone trying to find my space.

Homeroom is chaos, I'm trying to find my chair,
Avoiding stares and smoothing out my hair,
With teachers rambling on names I can't recall,
I feel like a fish in a classroom brawl.
Classes come and go, a whirlwind of faces,
Trying to keep up, tying mental laces,
First-day woes, they come and go,
But deep down, I'll let my confidence grow.

The bell rings, freedom at last,
Homebound, lessons learned, not just in class,
High school adventures, it's a wild ride,
First day jitters, but I'll take them in stride.

Pitch Perfect

In the arena, where the heart pounds,
Semi-finals fever, a boisterous crowd.
Balls colliding with bats, a fierce dance,
Hope and tension, at every fleeting glance.

On the pitch, under the sun's blazing caress,
Legends emerge, in a cricketing finesse.
Bats carve graceful arcs, a dance of willow and
leather,
Echoes of cheers erupt, such priceless moments
to treasure.

Bowlers, with eyes of fire, running in fast,
Fielders chasing dreams, their shadows cast,
In a sporting theater, emotions are on display.
In the semifinals drama, where champions play;

Cheers and screams, erupting in the air,
Every run, every wicker, a tale to share,
In this nail-biting moment, under the azure sky,
Celebrities are etched, as the stakes run high.

As the last ball sails, into victory's sweet
embrace,
The match is conquers, leaving a lasting trace,

Fans rejoicing, in the cricketing carnival,
On their road to glory where dreams can never
fall

Shadows Within

In the quiet corners of darkness, where shadows
lurk,
A heavy heart emerges, the struggles it shirks,
Demons dance, a silent scream,
In a world where life is a nightmare, not a
dream.

Darkness wraps around me, resembling a heavy
cloak,
Whispers of sadness, words unspoken,
unspoken,
Sorrow's weight, like a ball and chain,
Tying joy down, driving my soul insane

In this garden of despair, flowers droop,
Dreams and Hope, all tangles in a loop,
My heart, once a vibrant garden, now painted in
grey,
Where sunshine now seems so far away.

The sun plays hide and seek, such a timid game,
In a place where shadows and demons stake
their claim,
Silence sings, what a sombre song,
In my heart, where joy feels so wrong.

Yet, within the depths, a spark remains,
A tiny ember, despite the pains,
Through tear-stained eyes, it's a distant gleam,
A broken soul now starts to dream.

'Hang on, my friend,' a rhythm in time,
'Shadows can fade, your heart can transform,'
In my cocoon of pain, something rebirths,
A sunrise after the darkest mirth

Wild Whispers

Beneath the blue sky, where clouds float,
Nature throws a party, a whimsical gloat,
Trees tower over the ground, nature's
skyscrapers,
Swaying in the breeze, the ultimate shapers.

Raccoons play tag, a game of chase,
Birds gossip high up, in their personal space,
Tulips nod in the sun's warm glow,
As the river giggles, a liquid show.

Bees fly back and forth, in a pollen spree,
Butterflies flaunt their colours for all to see,
Dandelions launch their parachute flight,
A whimsy of wishes begins to take flight.

So to the wild, untamed, beautiful terrain,
Where every corner is a canvas, with something
to gain,
Mother Nature, the artist, with her brush so
grand,
Painting her masterpiece across the land.

Skybound Serenade

Up in the sky, I soar,
Through clouds and rain, I explore,
In comfy seats I sit in, with belts tight,
I'm ready for a wondrous, airborne flight

Engines hum, a jagged lullaby,
As we leap into the air, oh so high,
Tiny houses, like toys below,
As our plane begins to glow

People walk with carts in tow,
Snacks and drinks in a cheerful flow,
The turbulence shakes, what a bumpy ride,
But we're above the world, the clouds, side by
side

Peaking through the windows, I see the cities
gleam,
Rivers twist, a silver dream,
Above the clouds, where dreams take flight,
In this metal eagle, it's a soaring delight.

As we descent, with those wheels that spin,
Back to Earth, with a grateful,
A voyage shared, memories were made,
Flying high, in the sky, we played

Stellar soirée

Out in space, it's a crazy place,
Stars throw a glittery party in space,
Planets spinning, doing their thing,
In the supernatural disco, they dance and swing.

Mars, the cool cat, rocking red,
Venus struts by, turning heads,
Saturn with its rocky bling, like a celestial pop
star,
Jupiter the bouncer, the biggest by far.

The moon hangs around, with a sly grin,
Playing hide and seek, a mischievous twin,
Black holes, whispering secrets so hush,
In this spacey chaos, a celestial crush.

So let's stargaze, with wonder in our eyes,
Chase shooting stars, where the universe lies,
In this cosmic ballroom, where wonders abound,
We're just stardust beings, spinning around

Shadows within

In the quiet corners of darkness, where shadows lurk,
A heavy heart emerges, the struggles it shirks,
Demons dance, a silent scream,
In a world where life is a nightmare, not a dream.

Darkness wraps around me, resembling a heavy cloak,
Whispers of sadness, words unspoken, unspoken,
Sorrow's weight, like a ball and chain,
Tying joy down, driving my soul insane

In this garden of despair, flowers droop,
Dreams and Hope, all tangles in a loop,
My heart, once a vibrant garden, now painted in grey,
Where sunshine now seems so far away.

The sun plays hide and seek, such a timid game,
In a place where shadows and demons stake their claim,
Silence sings, what a sombre song,
In my heart, where joy feels so wrong.

Yet, within the depths, a spark remains,
A tiny ember, despite the pains,
Through tear-stained eyes, it's a distant gleam,
A broken soul now starts to dream.

'Hang on, my friend,' a rhythm in time,
'Shadows can fade, your heart can transform,'
In my cocoon of pain, something rebirths,
A sunrise after the darkest mirth